Coming home twice

Coming home twice

An Anthology of Verse
Maine Poets Society

Edited by
Margaret Rockwell Finch, Chairwoman
Anne W. Hammond
Joyce Pye
James B. Sargent
Lorna Starbird

ℳ𝒲ℬ
Just Write Books
Topsham, Maine, U.S.A.

Cover photos: Whale Rocks, Kennebec River
© Anne W. Hammond

All rights reserved.
Distributed by Just Write Books
47 Main Street #3, Topsham, Maine 04086
207-729-3600 • jstwrite@jstwrite.com
www.jstwrite.com
Book Orders: 207-729-3600

ISBN 0-9766533-3-8

Library of Congress Control Number:
2005929155

Dawn at Quoddy Head

Not as the prodigal son,
skulking home empty-hearted
across his father's fields;
nor even as the farm-bred feline
on noiseless paws, prowl-tired,
its night vigilance done;

But flamboyant, free,
astride its untamed steeds
of wave and tide
and accompanied by
the full orchestration
of an energizing sea,

Dawn hurtles itself once more
into the welcome embrace
of granite cliffs
to the thunderous applause
of a waiting shore.

———Mary R. Palmer

CONTENTS

SHADES OF DARKNESS

SECOND CHANCE

IF WE HAD A CHOICE

WATCHING

ANOTHER PERSPECTIVE

POSTHUMOUS POEMS

REVIEWS

This collection of poetry penned by members of the Maine Poets Society reflects the pace of life for which Maine is rightly famous. These are thoughtful poems that often celebrate the Maine landscape yet are deeply immersed in perennial human concerns. The carefully chosen words exist in relation to the powerful silences of the woods and water that define Maine. The variety of topics is impressive and so is the poets' dedication to their art. This is a fine representation of poetry from a venerable organization.

> Baron Wormser
> Maine Poet Laureate

Two poems each, chosen from the work of members of a society long devoted to the noble art of poetry, long rooted in the noble state of Maine—what a promise of variety and pleasure. Even if this book were not edited by my mother, I would have to say that it fulfills that promise. Here is a tribute worthy of the range of the art—with humor and pathos, lyric flights and wry observations—and the power of the place—with woods and barns, sheds and fishing boats, berries, birches, and a memorable fox.

> Annie Finch
> Poet, Director of the Stonecoast
> MFA Program in Creative Writing

PREFACE

I consider it an honor to preface this anthology since I am one of those who contributed to our first collection in 1948. Sixty-five people contributed to *As Maine Writes*, 106 pages of poetry. I still remember the gracious letter I received from Jessie Wheeler Freeman, an advisory committee member.

This is the 10th edition of the collective talent of Maine Poets Society writers, founded in1936. Originally called The Poetry Fellowship of Maine, the group united two mid-Maine poetic groups: Waterville Poetry Club and Dover-Foxcroft Poets Club.

The benefit of an anthology is to inspire all members to produce higher quality verse. And what better way to knit a tighter fabric of friendship than to invite new members?

The first meeting I was able to attend was in Brunswick at the Harriet Beecher Stowe House. Robert P. Tristram Coffin, a Bowdoin College professor, Poet in Residence, was our judge. I fell among the non-winners that day, but I always afterward heeded his succinct critique, " *'ings* are a lazy man's way to rhyme."

A rising member published in the first edition was Florence Burrill Jacobs, who wrote two books, *Stones and Other Poems*, and *Neighbors*. She contributed to our anthologies through 1971.

This little chore of writing a preface has opened my eyes to the value of anthologies for striving young poets. School children might relate to the poems of Maine Poets Society members who are learning just as they are. We are a grass-roots organization committed to the world of poetry.

Walter Field Sargent, Age 94
Auburn, Maine
2005

INTRODUCTION

If poetry is the art of having something to say, these voices of the Maine Poets Society are a welcome offering from diverse individuals. Sharing their insights are farmers, homemakers, students, teachers and a merchant sailor, college professors, historians, journalists, nurses, business people and visual artists. Their poetic inspiration stills the clamor of daily events before the timeless significance of personal experience.

The poems in this collection provide glimpses into modern perceptions of nature and wildlife, gardening, family heritage, and the human condition. Poets from age 16 to 94 speak on issues that engage them from true love and technology to abandonment and the habits of old folks. Voices of whimsy interface with somber elegy and sonnet query.

Our Society is committed to entertainment as well as constructive criticism. Form and subject contests establish the agenda for tri-annual meetings where work is read aloud and winners announced. Cash prizes leaven the day's events. Society meetings are a modern equivalent of ancient theatre in the round; think of us as wandering bards creating a venue for poetic expression.

To listen is to be inspired by the songs, trials, and courage of others. The poet's voice outstrips the raucous video-television world of noise and action riding roughshod over the intimate utterance of the human soul. In a world of terrorism replay, it is still the individual that speaks the loudest.

The Editors

Thus and so

THUS AND SO

The last time I hung fresh curtains
over the bedroom windows,
was the first day my husband
came home at 6 A.M.
Before that, he told me
he would be late
because of thus and so.

We did not speak,
and the toothpaste tasted of iodine.
As I opened a new can of coffee,
my stomach was a cat's cradle
waiting
to find a place for freezer pancakes.

My shoulders craved embrace,
and my mind needed penetration.
Through the kitchen window,
I could see a lone frog
floating
on a wrinkled sandwich bag
in an abandoned swimming pool.

———Lee Hutchins

dining in

seventy nine years—
      won't go out to a restaurant
—old

stubborn and stuck—
      just no need of it
—in his ways

married for sixty—
      never took his wife out to eat
—years

hundreds of thousands of—
      living in a trailer
—dollars tucked away

miserable miser doesn't mind if—
      restaurants are dirty
—his old wife complains

he'll die without trying—
      who knows who cooks that food
—a quarterpounder or a filet mignon

and his wife—
      when he's not looking
—just started going on her own

————Robin Merrill

DADDY IS ALWAYS RIGHT

Time and time again,
I find myself confined within these walls—
Where the oxygen slowly depletes,
And the gray clouds wrap themselves around my lungs.
They weave together to make a fist and squeeze tightly.
I suck for air, but suddenly it has disappeared.
There is nothing to breathe in
But the poison of Marlboro.
I raggedly make my way down the stairs
To find my daddy.
"Daddy, can I go out and play?"
He answers with a firm "No!"
I feel no need to interrogate.
Daddy knows what's best for me.
His glowing red-eyed frequent friend stares at me—
Laughing.
Daddy knows what's best for me.

———Shandi Kennedy-Robertson

NOT ANOTHER "SAPPY" LOVE POEM

Mesmerized
By the sound of your voice—
By your long, slender, delicately curved body.
Losing all focus as I glance your way,
I struggle to keep my composure.
In your presence,
I yearn to touch you—
To run my fingers along
Your neck, strategically.
I strive simply to
Pull your strings
And hear your sweet melodious
Moans.
Just to touch
That smooth cherry finish—
To strum along
Your fingerboard.
All day, I think about us together
Making passionate, love-ly
Music.

————Shandi Kennedy-Robertson

THE END OF PASSION

Post meridian. The cruel sun
Displays its majesty upon our heads.
Thank God our daily work is almost done
And we can totter to our hot damp beds.
There we will toss and moan and sulk and fret
In suffocating chamber and resist
Our spouse's clammy touch. For we forget
That on another day we even kissed.
But just before the dawn we feel a chill.
The sun's rage conquered, we again can reach
And show that love is really living still,
Past smoking lava, heated breath; and teach
Each other this affection, kinder far,
Like sweet spring mornings 'neath a milder star.

———Ann Kucera

REAPPEARANCES

It was said I had my mother's sensitivity
                              and my father's steadiness,
                              my mother's quickness
                    and my father's persistence
                    my mother's sociability
              and my father's sense of history
              my grandmother's sense of family
        and my grandfather's sense of whimsy
        my grandmother's way with handcrafts
and my grandfather's way with animals.

But my shyness
          stubbornness
                    inconsistencies
                              are Orphans.

————Earlene Ahlquist Chadbourne

APRIL

"Stars deprive the night of anonymity."
CONSTANCE HUNTING

I drive northward. Winter comes to meet
my car. Trees that promised buds below
are now stick-thin in wind. The sky is low,
as if darkness is its due. A frozen lake
gives up its ice. Black trees lie along
the water, crocodiles, tooth and tongue
on the wait, eyes alert for some mistake
of heart or mind. Not so long ago,
no, not so long, the August sky was wide
enough for all the stars that it could show
to open eyes, and we, along the tide
the hollow moon mistook for candle-flame,
sent the dark away to find another name.

———H. R. Coursen

AT CROW CALL

At early light when the crows called
you spread your arms out to the side
arched your back and raised your head
and you were lovely and raven and flying
and you took me with you holding tight
until the wind took your breath away
then gently brought you back to earth
the dark feathers of your emotion fading
into earthy form and dreamy sleep.

———Arnold Perrin

Pinching pickles

PINCHING PICKLES

Five years older, a brother type,
my uncle led me to the bulkhead,
then down into the house's mouth
deep below the lawn.

There, a sprawling peoples' mouse hole
with bouldered, earth-packed walls,
low ceilinged, and musty-cozy,
garden bounty neatly shelved.

The flat-caked floor threw dust
when I jumped, spiders raced to webs.
No echo offered for Grandma's ears,
her harvest treasure entered.

The egg grader's hum
hid our grunts and groans
as we strained to pry
sealed lids from gallon jars.

We raided and crunched the puckering punch,
all sizes of mustards and dills.
Olive green long boiled and brined
we tasted–and sampled the lot.

A creak from above, the signal to leave
in quick, kid-speed retreat
to granite steps that led up and out
cooling our bare summered feet.

———Deborah Neumeister

EQUINOX, MATINICUS ISLAND

I.

When the moon flies over my shoulder
and daylight comes too fast,
I stand on earth
thin among round stones
washing downrock to the sea.

Flying moons, shoulders, boulders
rolling past, too fast, two nights
roll together, spring to spring.

Moon flown over the island
rocking in the sea
wait to see who will live.

II.

Where stories stand, thick and honest
as old Christmas wreaths on shed doors,
but not necessarily true,
families wrap roots, wires and vines
around the school yard, church yard
and into boats out for fish
looking out for each lonely house
binding lives and deaths, cleaving hearts
together under wind, alee.

———Sharon Bray

WAGON WAY

The old highway plunged into pine woods
for two hundred years, past bogs and into the river valley
taking travelers north to riches and fame
in the woodlots and quarries of Maine.

We turn into the diminishing dirt lane,
but our high-tech machine slows to a crawl
where a missing culvert cross-ditched the way.
A great house and barn crouch on the curve of the hill;

some past resident celebrated success with bargeboard
and loop trim. We imagine a wagon laden with milk
driving out of the barn, oxen urged onward
by the calloused hands that coaxed harvest from stony land.

On a slow roll, our vista shrinks: minted flowers bloom
on spring's slope, ferns unfold beneath the canopy
of pale leaves. Warbler song fills the scented breeze.
A puddle the size of a pond masks the mud beneath,

stalling our car. The wagon would have slowed,
the animals struggled, but the load would have moved on,
mud an impassable part of progress. Blocked by
technology, we step out, ready to try the wagon way.

———Anne W. Hammond

LANGUAGE

for Alex

If you're gonna understand,
let me explain: around these here parts
people communicate with truck horns.
Depending on duration, pattern, frequency,
a series of honks can say:
    —Haven't seen you in a while.
    —Excited now to see you.
    —Goin' to town, be right back.
    —Goin' by your house now, thought you'd like to know.
    —My father honks to you so I do too.
    —Fuck you.
    —Fuck you too.
The most versatile language,
with minimal effort
we honk our way through these small towns
never thinking anything of it.
Now, you'll understand my surprise
when my friend asked me
why I was honking to the cemetery on the Kingfield road
long, loud, laboriously, with rhythm
and who the hell I was honking to
and now you'll understand
how much sense it made to both of us when I said
I was just sayin' hi to my dad.

———Robin Merrill

SOMETHING THERE IS ABOUT MAINE

that draws her native-born children back to her breast
like homing pigeons to the roost. Before losing
the superior knowledge of adolescence, I vowed
to leave forever this remote, unsophisticated
dead end of the world.

Growing up in the heart of Maine, I knew autumn
flame reflected in pewter waters, winter windswirls
of snow whooping through white fields of cold, rising
spring waters on glacier-abandoned river boulders,
scent of new-cut hay drying in heat haze of summer.

Growth was measured by each setting sun moving
patiently through seasons from Guilford Notch to
elephant-backed Borestone Mountain and back again.
I did not know it wasn't marrow in my bones, but essence
of the land I wanted to flee.

Like a slow-motion boomerang arcing through years
of Boston, Chicago, Los Angeles, curving to Kansas plains,
Amish country, D.C., I returned–inevitably–to Maine.

What calls us back? Roots, our own and others',
the participatory democracy of town meeting,
and the people. Neighbors seldom seen until trouble,
when they come out of their lives to give aid and comfort,
to stay on your side of the road, to walk the extra mile.

There's a sense of presence here. You can feel
earlier lovers of this special land–the Red Paint people,
Abenakis, first settlers, John Adams as a youthful
circuit lawyer riding, riding . . .

And above all . . . the intangible something
of the soul beyond expression that
a true Mainer understands.

———Jeanette K. Cakouros

HOMING

What is it in my veins
that sings at
wash of wave
and sea smell,
that inland pond
and lake disdains,
that clings to
coastal strand,
however beautiful
the land?

I only know I must go
where ocean's swell
and seabirds' cries
echo down
long reaches under
windswept skies,
where tide's ebb
and flood
find the pulse beat
in my blood.

———June A. Knowles

SUMMER COMMUNION

Remember the ripeness of Summer's days
and how, after all Spring greenness had passed,
we stood at last within hot August's steaming dark
watching far-away flickers of lightning
and fireflies flying so close
we could almost touch them;
how they cast an eerie light on skies so stark and black,
blacker than blackberries, blacker that the day was bright.
And, oh! how the crickets sang long in the night.

Now elderberry wine was in the making
and all raking the rolling blue barrens
had since been done. And, yes! how we'd won
the summer competition for best raspberry jam
and gone to greatness in our grandchildren's eyes
with cranberry bread and berry pies so holy that, to them,
we ought to bake them again in the skies.
And how, back in June, in that now-gone meadow
we'd discovered his blood in strawberries.
"Take, eat," he'd said. "Do this in remembrance . . . "

————James B. Sargent

Reflections

REFLECTIONS

I.

The boulder stands above still water
Ancient, unchangeable.
The image wavers
Shatters
In a weightless riffle of wind.

II.

Sun sparks on smooth water
Brilliance disembodied.
Fire and water,
Energy and repose.
Weightless and dazzling,
Visible, invisible, indivisible.

III.

That spark glowing on the water
Does not necessarily mean that my neighbor across the river
Has lit her kitchen window, as I have mine.
It is only reflection from window to water,
The first rays of sun shining a pool of light
Which will change from gold to white
Expand to the intensity of a galactic explosion
Then dwindle and vanish
As the bright morning disc appears
Over the black ridge of hills to my east.

————Betty King

HALF NOTES

The
music
gently
weaves
around
my
soul
like
rib-
bons
in the
wind.
Care-
free   black
notes   fall like
leaves   without
direction   an old song
waiting   in the
shadows   of my
        mind.

———Jean Blodgett

VICTORY

Remember when she mastered that two-wheeler?
    Her knees were scabbed for weeks, as I recall.
But, oh, the pride in that announcement:
    "I did it! And I didn't even fall!"

The times she'd taken spills no longer counted;
    Success made every bit of pain worthwhile.
"I really did it!" This she kept repeating.
    And everyone who heard her had to smile.

At times when I am faced with problems
    And disturbed by life's complexities,
I take courage from that cherished memory
    Of a child with shining eyes and banged-up knees.

—————Sally R. Joy

LEGACY OF STONE

Whenever I see a stone wall
    I marvel at the toil,
The struggle of early farmers
    As they tried to till the soil.
I reflect on how those brave men
    Battled pain to clear the land,
The price they paid to sow that seed
    Where you and I now stand.
Fields, framed with stone, are everywhere,
    From sea to mountain, and beyond,
While the Pioneers who cleared them,
    Our forefathers, are gone.
To me it seems inappropriate,
    Now they are dead,
That we find them lying there in fields
    With stones above their heads.

————Bill Lindie

EASTWARD

My tattered spirit found a place,
and followed round the bend
to manor made with charm and grace,
where past and now might blend.

Oaks stand guard against the world;
they call the house their mother.
Birches cling in clusters,
whispering secrets to each other.

To the west a meadow,
and there a little pond.
A heron keeps his vigil;
the mountain lies beyond.

Sun-dipped days and star-blind nights,
eastward lies the sea
where fishers fish and sailors sail,
sometimes just for me.

I watch and mend, where ocean meets the rocks
to leave its foam.
Peace enters through my window eyes,
and makes itself at home.

———Ina Doban

SURVIVAL

Violence fills the earth
and a president is wounded
while young blacks still die
                (yet a bird sings).

Two men die of starvation
martyrs to an old cause,
The Holy Father is shot
                (yet the grass grows).

Wars erupt in a restless world
and needlessly men perish
for the greed of nations
                (yet there is hope).

———Lorna Starbird

HOYA PLANT

No night moth or kiss of wind
in this quiet place
only I enticed
to climb the sweet-scented stairs
and offer my beating heart
in the window of the moon.

————Arnold Perrin

QUIETUDE

I have friends who are uncomfortable
                    with quiet–
and seem compelled
                    to fill each moment
                    with sounds

perhaps   silence   was a tool of   anger
            or   intimidation   in their childhood–
for them now to be so
            disquieted   with   quiet

they've   missed   the   pristine   beauty   of a   world
                    moving in stillness–

                    resonating in silence–
            an aria staged   without   applause.

———Earlene Ahlquist Chadbourne

AMERICA AT MIDNIGHT

From our orbital eye in space
east and west are all awash with
light as if the invisible ocean's
blind waves were breaking there, a surf
suffused with phosphorescent life.
While in the heartland, on the wide
dark plains, only scattered cities shine
like constellations of pale stars.

We imagine lines connecting,
lines that might be rail or highways.
Lines making patterns in the mind
from which imagination shapes
fantastic forms: here an Indian
with a bow, there a Buffalo.

————Robert M. Chute

Shades of darkness

SHADES OF DARKNESS

You come to me in silent memories
Of spring, in growing things and gentle rain.
Warm nights embrace old passions, fill a breeze
With apple-blossom fragrance to sustain
Emotions. Under moonlit trees outside,
An orchard, where we often walked and planned
Our future. Years together were denied;
I watched you slip away and held your hand.
In spring I walk the shadowed paths beneath
White branches, petals fall–caress my cheek–
Creating rings around my feet, a wreath
Of love, a joyous gift I did not seek.
In shades of darkness, you appear with schemes
To fill the empty corners of my dreams.

———Earla Towne Nelson

FOR SKIPPER

On this hill of peace
above the river,
a piper calls us to a last sharing
on a soft May afternoon.
Bare trees of a Maine spring
and a shore still winter sere
frame the Bagaduce.

On this green hill
rimming town and sea,
taps sounds, the last note floating
on a salt breeze
as a falling tide runs down river
to sing a bright spirit
on his way.

Evening light floods Windy Hill,
gilds mowed fields
and weathervane,
silhouettes the barn.
Clouds flame westward
while Drift, beloved border collie,
patrols¾guarding, grieving¾
sensing safe harbor
for his master's
last good voyage.

——————June A. Knowles

CENTER MORICHES 1941

I want to replace in Center Moriches
those who lived here before.
I want to move them back
to yellow and brown colored Depression houses
on Lake Avenue, Senix Avenue, Clinton Street.
I want Tom, Al, Bob back
where I can find them, answering phones
that no longer ring.
I want these families—still young—
living out lives in solid houses
lining Chichester Avenue, Canal Street, Ocean Avenue.
I want to buy back that twilight hour of December 27,
when Warren and Claude sipped their last cherry coke
on valentine-shaped wire chairs
at Pete's candy store.
I want to buy back time,
whisper goodbye to
those nine who became
the faded, yellow-crackled snap-shot grief
of World War II.

Carlos Adams   Warren Dayton
Alfred Fehner   Kurt Hartman
Thomas O'Conner   John Prosser
Vernon Robinson   Robert Ross
              Claude Schuyler

————Lee Hutchins

ARCTIC TERN

We saw the Arctic tern by chance
on a beach in northern France.
Here to summer, we were told,
escaping from Arctic cold.
We ran and rode in summer sun,
played until time began to run
down the hourglass of sand.
Time to return to our own land.
Through all our life thereafter,
between tears and laughter
we always hoped to see
the Arctic tern flying free.
But death took you on ahead.

One bleak day my footsteps led
to a Cape Cod beach in misty gray
on a windy, storm-tossed bay.
Suddenly over the surf I heard
beating wings of the Arctic bird.
Looking up, my grieving heart
knew we would never be apart.

———Lorna Starbird

WAR GAMES

It's a curious place, my garden;
a battle zone of life and death.
In Spring, it's more like a cemetery than anything,
with loved ones carefully buried, then left to rest.
Arlington's like that. One is struck by the precision of the rows,
like a cornfield with stalks of crosses. The difference,
of course, is that nothing will grow there.

Then comes the enemy invasion.
No time for smart bombs or precision-guided
artillery fire now. This hoeing is old-fashioned
hand-to-hand combat. In the process, I'll accidentally
chop off the head of a new-born bean or two.
The military has a term for that one;
it's called collateral damage.

After a few guerilla attacks by those insidious insect sects,
I'll pull out my trusty duster. Talk about chemical warfare!
And isn't this the epitome of ethnic cleansing?
But what if some ladybugs die? I guess that's what one
must expect from (how can it be?) "friendly fire."

As the season winds down we gather our spoils
(before *they* do) and go home, only to return
with the tiller—our favorite weapon of mass destruction—
to prepare the plot for burials next Spring.

————James B. Sargent

THE HEALER

from *Verses on the Margin of a Field-map*

A coppery shield hangs low
In the slate gray sky
As a glowing buckler
Giving no warmth
Or protection.
A pale mist hangs over the battlefield
  drifting over the field of no honor,
  driving a breeze that isn't there.
A thin man in white drifts among the wounded and dying
  touching here, speaking there,
  always moving, ever staying.
The form is shrouded
  The hands glow and dance
  ever moving, ever still
  deftly caring, healing, caressing, easing.
The voice like velvet steel
  comforts, reassures, eases, strengthens.
Those that must die he strengthens,
  Those that must live he consoles.
Those that the Maker has neither called nor sent,
  he soothes.

In delirium's sway, this field becomes the world.
This healer becomes the only answer.

The blanket of the night spreads its succor
        over the bleeding wounded land
        and the healer is gone
yet stays 'til the universe stops
stays until the "warrior's bow shall be banished."[1]

Another time, another field waits for him.
Bloody fields spread over time and space–needing him.
The coppery moon ascends like a dented shield,
A chill breeze carries the scent of carnage
        and memory of caring.
The jagged hill's peaks become city's jutting towers.

The dying man feels the wings of the dove
        despite pain's insistence and fear's iron hold–
        he smiles . . .

————Erik Christian

---

[1] Zec. 9/9-10

WHEN DEATH COMES

When Death comes sneaking,
to jump on my chest and
thrust his dagger
of white light between my eyes;
when Death comes,
with his bristles and moaning bells;
when Death comes
tinkling like the spring wind upon the Prairie;
I want to step boldly through
the crack between the Worlds,
knowing already
what it's going to be like,
to lift up the edge of the Sky
and drift forever—
cradled in the loving embrace of
immaculate white light—
my spirit floating as free as thistledown
on the dawn wind of space.

I want to look upon all of my life
as rainbows and thunder,
and all time as a sunset,
and see eternity as the blinking of God's eye,
and I will remember
each of my friends,
as rare and as singular
as a nocturnal flower;

and each friend's name
as a fruit picked
at the peak of ripeness;
and each of my loved ones
as an angel
fallen preciously to Earth.

And when it's over,
I want to be able to say:
"All my life I rode
the whirlwinds of amazement,
taking the whole Universe
into my soul–
I don't want to wonder
if I have made of my life
something useful and real,
or find myself
frightened and sighing–
wondering why I never
fully inhaled this amazing World."

after Mary Oliver

————Paul Averill Liebow

Second chance

SECOND CHANCE

Though predictable,
the hurricane of widowhood
swept upon her
in an unexpected
and disorienting rush.
In its eye
she faced emancipation,
sensing there was more to truth.

She tallied up her loss
and, of a sudden, saw
must savor, too, the gain.
Days of summers gone,
those drugged or clamorous hours
previously composed
of pokey stops and starts
became nights barely long enough.

Late in the dark
new companions came,
seduced to her bed
from a dusty shelf of games:
Frost, Newman, Eliot, Yeats,
an endless line of suitors.
She took to writing poems
under several assumed names.

———Helen Streeter Kelly

OUT TO DRY

It seems I've been hung out to dry,
crinkle-clipped at both shoulders
on some washer woman's frayed
                    braided line,

aflap in a stiff confused breeze.
Too long in a fine recollection
and wantin' to get on with it,
                    I pine,

impatient for collection.
I am ready to be gathered in,
shaken briskly with a furl
                    and a snap,

folded up, pressed neat and tight,
so's even I know where I fit
in a crowded drawer called
                    everyday life.

—————Helen Streeter Kelly

ABANDONED

Sally went home today
As I rocked in Father's chair.
They came and told me,
Their voices far away.
Sally went home today
Forgetting all our plans.
Now I sit in Father's chair
Correcting all our dreams
While watching the sunset
On just another day.

————Jean Blodgett

I'VE ALWAYS DANCED

I was Bostonized for education, enlightened
from tap dancing and pink pirouettes *en pointe*
to parks gathering the karma of flute-playing hippies,
waving bodies and clapping hands, bearing
tin-clinking, twanging tambourines toward the subway.

I pranced joyously in my East Indian skirt,
tinkling my tiny bells and glass, evil-eye buttons.
I bounced to pounding drummers jamming at the half shell,
dressed to portray some inner fringe
rocking out and beginning to fray; colored beads

and embroidered butterflies pretended to scout
flowers on the cuffs of my jeans.
I hummed the climate of the Common;
a mosaic fit between gawking squares and purple people,
until the cops came on horseback, scattering

the head-banded crowd in dizzying directions.
I tightened my bandana and cocked out my thumb,
let wind finger my mane into long strands
of sunflower gold whipped by the Harley's draft;
that bike zig-zag-doesy-doed me out of there.

I hitch-hiked an atlas of miles with the heart of a mustang,
restless to roam, until the night I arrived on a moonlit field
to star gaze and waltz through tall timothy
in the arms of a lover.

———Deborah Neumeister

YARD SALE

Bits of me
scatter
among friends and foes
and strangers.

Rummaged
hand through hand,
to settle
in houses and schools
and landfills.

There,
seagulls
and pickers
are happier than ever
to have me.

—————Victoria Eastman

A SHORT PLAY

No one tells you how fast it goes,
the feeling you can do anything—
the marriage, the children, all that love

That suddenly vanishes.
The play is over, the curtain drawn,
the house dark, and you wend your way out

Alone into the street, without a home—
without a real home, just empty rooms.
No one tells you how the years will stretch out

And the memories won't seem real.
They lie. The memories don't feel good.
They're stabs in the gut.

Replaying them
is like watching television
in a dark room,

A dim sputter of light,
a slow burning out of a candle,
and it goes on for a very long time—

The dying of the bright dancing drama
of youth, now merely a short play
in your mind.

———Yamile Craven

REALIZATION DISABILITY

When I see that time has passed,
evident by loss, gained wisdom,
weary sighs, mirrored looks which
tell me nothing lasts,
I am amused I sometimes
feel surprise.

(As though my peers could amble down
the lane while I just stayed behind
to dance a while.
Empathy might help me feel their
pain, but I could laugh along
yet another mile.)

Yet as I walked and danced,
youth left me behind, music
fading, movements soon to cease.
Amazing!
Not that this could be,
but that I found it so hard
to believe.

————Ina Doban

If we had a choice

IF WE HAD A CHOICE

Today is not a good day to die;
no birds on high; no sun in the sky.
This is not a good day to die.

Tomorrow is a better day to die;
it has not come yet, you see.

This day will flee over the rim
of the world and tomorrow
will come up out of the sea
but tomorrow it will not be
because it will be today, you see.

Tomorrow might be a good day to die.
But you won't see it and neither will I
because by then it will be today
and today is not a good day to die.

————Bernard Ryer

MISGUIDED

Sprinkle-spit.
The Lord pokes fun
at our heat wave.

Twenty
discernible drops
hit the windshield.

One
tiny, cool kiss
inadvertently placed
on my cheek.

————Victoria Eastman

DO IT YOURSELFER

My stomach churns!
I hide from you,
You, who are installing
A modern convenience,
Wrecking havoc
On my kitchen.
You cut my sideboard,
Block one cupboard,
Remove the door from another
With no hope of replacement.
You call me to see
Where you've torn the tiling.
My heart jumps
But I smile.
You are proud because
With this, your gift,
I'll never have to suffer
From dishpan hands again.

—————Rosalie Doughty

ENDEARMENT

SMILING, STANDING
IN THE DOORWAY
YOU WATCH ME
WHILE I
PULL
TUG
PUSH
ZIP
SNAP
BUTTON
COMB
BRUSH BLUSH.
YOU SAY WORDS
WIVES NEED TO HEAR,
"HURRY UP, WE'RE LATE."

————Rosalie Doughty

WINTER NIGHTS

When winter snow begins to fall
All the snowplows have a ball.
Dancing lights begin to play
Around the room in grand display.
The night becomes alive with sound;
Noisy motors all around,
Up the street, down the roads
And in the yards with bucket loads.
Move the snow they must, you know,
For busy humans on the go.
So let the snowplows have their ball
When winter snow begins to fall.

————Julia Ward

FLOWER TALK

Walking through the fields one day
Thoughts of war were dark and gray.
A sad, sad world it seemed to be
Until a Brown Eyed Susan winked at me.

———Julia Ward

GOING ONCE

...GOING TWICE

...GOING...GONE!

There is a bit of fascination
Mixed with thoughts of expectation,
As the crowd amasses in the auction hall.

It is a proof of validation,
Spider marks of desecration,
In the faded chamber pot that's near the wall.

Auctioneer shows adoration
By his practiced titillation,
"It's the rarest of the rarest of the rare!"

Some will show their agitation
With no art appreciation,
While the bidders bid, they show they know and care.

There is no prestidigitation,
And no show of desperation,
As he adds an ancient yellowed silk chiffon.

With an excited stimulation,
Fear and hope in undulation,
It is going, it is going and it's gone.

———Ernestine F. Bent

TASTEFUL

I'd like my thoughts to be

an airy cream-puff flavor . . .

vanilla is the best for me,

with a taste of chocolate later.

And if my mind won't stand for this,

I'll really have to try

to change my ways,

and think of things

like tangy lemon pie!

—————Ernestine F. Bent

WHEN

Spring happens with fits and starts,
Borrows a day here and there,
Slips in to nudge roots and buds
From hibernation.

Southeasterly breeze carries
Scents of spring over layers of snow,
Prods ol' Sol to lift from winter couch
To rise high above trees.

On south face of the barn
Swords of ice grow and break,
Drop to stand like dancers
en pointe.

Snow draws back
From warm corners of the house;
Rowdy crocuses appear.
Outrageous colors of
Pink, purple and orange
Announce loudly
Spring is here!

A collective sigh
Sweeps through the valley,
Even enters the village store:
Ah . . . spring at last.
Maybe.

———David L. Davis

ALPHABET SEED

A bright, snappy October day
Finds grandboys poking around
Hoo Hoo's frost-ravaged pumpkin patch.
Orange globes shoulder through
Crumbled brown leaves and flaccid vines
Beckoning eager hands' quest.

"Hoo Hoo, this pumpkin
Has Zeke's name on it," calls Prescott.
Curtis tumbles over as he tugs his pumpkin free.
"Check them over carefully," I intone,
"The harvest is special this year."
"I can't believe my name is on
this huge one," says Lewis.
"Here's mine," chuckles Dave.
"Have you found your pumpkin, Pres?" asks Zeke.
"Yep, it's a dandy and Ginny has a beauty, too."
Hoo Hoo calls, "Better gather them up boys,
It's getting late. Halloween is tomorrow night."

"Hoo Hoo, how can this be?" they all ask,
"Our names growing on these pumpkins?
"Is it magic?"
A twinkle of eyes, a quiet smile upon his lips,
Hoo Hoo admits planting
Alphabet seed.

———David L. Davis

Watching

WATCHING

A white cat for all seasons,
just past the garden
settles on a dusted crust of snow,
licks his paws, ready
for any mouse who might
creep out of snowbent straw.

————Sharon Bray

THE FOX

Of the many things
the fox knew
one was precision
her tract
stretched straight
across new snow

one was the pounce
front feet
pinning the vole
in the grass

one was suddenly
doing nothing
standing unseen
in plain sight

one was style
leaping the wall
her tail as bold
as Mae West's boa

these are only
a few of the things
the fox knew

————Robert M. Chute

RHUBARB IN RAIN

I stalk the wily rhubarb
Under elephant ears of leaf
Machete in hand.

There may be tigers!
Never have I seen
This simulacrum of jungle

In our hard-scrabble garden
Which last year at this time
Was parched and dry.

Today I forage like a pygmy
Dwarfed by vegetation
Surrounded by food.

————Betty King

WAIT FOR ME

You are dapple-dream, golden dog—
      Sleeping in puddled sun under hemlocks,
      Inhaling sweetgrass scent and autumn days.

If you run in young abandon,
      Wait for me.
      Wait for me!

You are reverie of homecoming, golden dog.
      You color gray surroundings,
      Friend of dove song early evenings.

When the wind stirs thought of running,
      Wait for me.
      Wait for me!

————Anita Liberty

YOU'LL SEE ME AGAIN

You'll see me again when birds sing from bended twig,
and butterflies embroider the day.
You'll see me again when the moon performs her magic
and draws the ocean's waters up against the beach.
You'll see me again when little kittens play
and an oriole sings about the newness of the day.
You'll see me when, like a string of beads,
little ducklings follow in their mother's wake.
You'll see me when a puppy looks at you for comfort
and cicadas make their music on a warm, summer night.
You'll see me again when wild geese trail
their discordant cries across the sky,
    and a loon call quavers across the lake,
proclaiming the exuberance of life.
You'll see me when sandpipers tiptoe the beach
then turn to escort the new wave
as it washes up a fresh supply of food.
You'll see me when chickadees cock their heads
to look at you as you fill their feeder with seed
and I'll be there when someone has a desperate need.
You'll see me again when life is deep, and sad, and dark;
I'll reach out to you from the filmy dust of eternity
    and you will know I am there.
You'll see me again.

————Bernard Ryer

MANTIS MODE

What have we here?
Detected in the grass
(Plant and creature nearly one
In spare green symmetry),

We use the Greek for *prophet*,
Enchanted by its
"Stout anterior legs
Like hands folded in prayer."

But—wait a minute!

Eternal paradox:
We're sometimes moved to change
That letter *a* to *e*,
Seeing how skillfully

It uses prayer
To spring upon its prey:

Not unlike
We who observe.

—————Margaret Rockwell Finch

BLUE-WHITE FEBRUARY

A world dressed
in shades of white
lies under an
ice-blue sky.
Feet frozen
in drifts, black
trees stand naked
in the wind
and shiver around
the corner of February
into spring.

—————Earla Towne Nelson

AFTER AN AUTUMN DRIVE

Leaves, leaves, fragile, rattling leaves!
Restless moments verged on passing . . .
Still, across memory's screen,
a red-gold mix
tumbles down macadam ways,
colorful cider-spill
fresh from the press of time.
Hills and valleys are October mellow,
richly mulled by summer's strife.
A muted leaf-crunch lulls me now
breathless falling out . . . quiet rustle,
lazy down-sliding spiraling leaf-fall
that covers my technicolor dream and me.

————Walter Field Sargent

Another perspective

ANOTHER PERSPECTIVE

from an antique window

A leaf falls from
My venerable tree–
Small and yellow, falling
Into this my autumn,

But my catching breath discovers
Another's autumn lost and long
Ago, the curtain caught aback
From open window by–whose hand?

Hers–not mine, where she leans
Watching, waiting, her young tree
Inside my old tree she uncovers
Where my air trembles through her leaves–

One is small and yellow, falling
Through the air not mine but hers.

Will, one day, another woman find me
Leaning, waiting–and wonder in a breath
Who this may be, her hand upon the curtain,
Watching the autumn tree not hers but mine?

———Margaret Rockwell Finch

YARD SALE BOX

Red and yellow tulips, green stalks,
painted on a lacquered dark green box.
A small round box that I picked up,
turned round and round
and then set down.

Its bottom is veneered in black
and shows no artist's name.
A hand unwavering edged its lid
with a thin gold line.
And then the vee
cut in the middle of a tulip
to fit lid to box cleverly.

"I'll take it," said I,
handing owner two dollars.
"A ninety-year-old lady," she said,
"made that."

Sparkling tulip box,
now filled with cough drops,
you show me modesty
and undiminished artistry.
You tell me beauty
has its own reason to be.

———Yamile Craven

TREASURE

I am a thief of love, whose greedy eye
Seeks out the treasure in another's store,
Who snatches it without receipt, unseen
Devours it and hurries back for more.

If love is sold on countertops for gold
Or reputation or expediency,
Then I have robbed and broke the law,
But rather would I thief, than buyer be.

Who buys such goods and pays hard cash
Buys nothing, though he adds his heart to boot.
Spendthrift exchange! Better a Vandal be
And flee with arms entwined in precious loot.

But love will not be held as property,
Subject to barter, argument or stealth,
To rapine, violence, contract or loss;
But currency from an eternal wealth

That circulation polishes and hoarding dims.
It is a bank where savings shrink, and door
Unlatched, invites the thief and prodigality
Inside to chafer and increase its store.

————Ann Kucera

COMING HOME TWICE

I dreamed of light and warmth,
a welcome note, a sliver of love
slipped under the door.
                    A basket of eggs or
                    violets licked with dew.

But the house was dank and dark,
wet news slung against the sill,
ficus humbled with neglect,
                    silence echoing farewell.

Then tissue torn, kindling split,
a long match drawn, the kettle set.
Mozart tuned, sheet turned,
pillow fluffed, clock keyed
to *my* time:
                    Midnight.

Hour of alchemy
Infusion of rosemary
Rich ripe hickory
Flicker of candlelight
Roses pressed on porcelain cup.

I almost believed it was waiting.

———Joyce Pye

THE SHEPHERD

My poem roams round the borders of my mind
Scouting the perimeters–
Sniffing at weeds, frisking an ant,
Lifting a leg.

Ears pricked, his compass tuned for
Blizzard's wailing winds, a flock astray,
He rounds me up, sheep wandering with wolves
    Outside the boundaries.

———Joyce Pye

POTENTIAL

What is a seed?
It's gift-wrapped potential.
An object so tiny
You can cradle it in your palm.
Yet under its protective outer shell
Rest promises of growth
And future generations.
A gift-wrapped miracle—that's a seed.

What is a dream?
It's very like a seed.
And so it may continue to exist—tiny,
Not spectacular to look at.
Yet under its protective outer shell
Are promises restless for release.
Wish-wrapped potential—
That's a dream.

Not all seeds grow.
Not all dreams are realized.
Potential must be planted,
Nurtured,
Warmed and watered into being.
You would not place dry seed upon a shelf
And look for it to sprout.
What are you doing with your dreams?

———Sally R. Joy

TRANSPOSED

I sit and sip this water . . .
Gazing into the glass . . .
My mind deep in thought
Of days long passed . . .

Where has this water been . . .
Since the beginning of time . . .
What journey has it taken . . .
Before becoming mine?

Has it flowed down the Nile . . .
With Cleopatra's barge . . .
Or floated the North Atlantic . . .
As an iceberg . . . oh, so large?

Has it soared . . .high in a cloud . . .
Out where those trade winds blow?
Did it form perfect crystals . . .
Have I shoveled them as snow?

Has it nourished each grape,
As it ripened on the vine?
Was it present at "That Wedding" . . .
Where Jesus changed it to wine?

Ah . . . . What lovely water.
Refreshed . . . I finger the glass . . .
Still reflecting on its journey
In those days . . . long passed.

———Bill Lindie

VERGE OF LIFE

"A wind ripple may
transform itself into life."
　　　　　　LOREN EISELEY,
　　　　　　IMMENSE JOURNEY

First life . . . fragile, emergent creation
(death but enhances its worth).
What tremulous incarnation
quickened mere cells to birth?

In what eon of slime and ooze,
by what ordering of vapor and sun
did ferment and stagnation lose
to the will of life begun?

Dredge the deep for an answer,
tunnel and crawl under ground,
scan the stars for a vision,
listen in space for a sound,

still, life's high mystery pervades
the land, the sky and the sea:
that precious gift of creation,
that unquenchable *will* to be.

————Walter Field Sargent

BLUES FOR MR. BLAKE

You set that Tyger all on fire,
You made that Tyger glow with fire,
And launched those arrows of desire.

You watered London with your tears,
The streets of London ran with tears.
The marriage-hearse ran down the years.

And England's green and pleasant hills,
Yes, those green and pleasant hills
Were shadowed by satanic mills.

And chimney sweepers rose like sheep,
Yes, children rose at dawn like sheep,
And soon enough lay down to sleep.

And through the forests of the night,
Through all the woodlands of the night,
That Tyger still is shining bright.

————H. R. Coursen

ODE TO THE SAGADAHOC BRIDGE

Glass
by the light
of the river reflecting silver
on the gleaming, graceful arch
that stretches from left bank far out into fog
toward infinity where men cling like fleas to tons
of man-made stone and barges belly up with more
to gird the bully builders for the climb to even greater heights.
Cast to surpass all probable stress, polished to seal the power,

concrete bound with steel filaments is designed to conquer time.
Men buttress segment against segment, erecting a monument
to movement, a wonder we worship like the thousands
of vehicles that will pass over to dream destinations
and beyond. Grand is the span; indomitable,
record-breaking, a test of geological time
when it will crack
and fall like
glass.

————Anne W. Hammond

THE GLASS COCOON

Who will rehearse the lullaby
In this pristine nursery
For the infinitesimal hybrid
Lovelessly inseminated
In a crystal womb?
Seedling exposed
To the analytical eye
Of an expectant surrogate
Who pencils the growing process
And cultivates life
In a garden of ampules
Rooted to stainless steel,
A transplanted ideal
For the discriminating client
Demanding perfection
And ignoring the fine print
On the bill of sale:

*"Due to the extreme fragility of the spirit,
we cannot guarantee the content of this package."*

———Anita Liberty

Posthumous poems

VERMEER'S *THE MILKMAID*

Forget the composition just for now.
Don't think of brush strokes, nor the way
The colors harmonize. Consider how
The artist felt and what he had to say.
Why did he choose an everyday event?
See sunlight coming through the window pane
To touch her face so tenderly. She is intent
Upon her task, not tempted to complain.
She knows the worth of what she does. The sweet,
Cool milk she pours, the crusty, new-baked bread,
Highlighted by the artist, will complete
The simple meal by which her world is fed.
In food, in life, in art, he makes us see
The lasting beauty of simplicity.

——————Mary Helen Georgitis

SUBJECT AND ARTIST–*THE PORTRAIT*

No longer young and never beautiful
She stands there at the outer edge of time
And knows herself far less desirable
Than once she was, acknowledges the crime
Of age, if crime it is to live too long
And love that life too much to let it go.
The artist sees her feet both planted strong
Upon the earth she loves–he does not know
Nor care to know, the bitter way she sees
Herself. Her graceless posture is to him
Symbolic of her strength. His aim is not to please
The current taste nor satisfy the public whim
But to show truth–so she, by his success,
Has passed, through art, from time to timelessness.

––––––Mary Helen Georgitis

THE CONDIMENT

Their condiment in scant supply was time.
Its snippets, gleaned from summer's laboring hours,
Were served on golden plates by setting sun
To farmer and his wife on weathered porch,
Relaxed to watch their fields slip into night.

Blue halos rose above his corncob pipe
To hover briefly, scatter and dissolve.
He'd talk of haying, hoeing, and report
How young fruit trees were faring on the hill.

Her apron left on hook by kitchen door,
She'd smooth her gingham dress and try to firm
The bun of dark hair resting on her neck.
She'd speak a little of her busy day
With winter's food set boiling in its jars
Atop a hungry woodstove, jungle heat
Attacking her resolve and losing out.
For moments, words unsaid hung on the air
Fraught with dreams of Someday and Somehow.

At last, she would complain that pesky gnats
Were getting to her and she'd best go in.
Then he would grin and offer her his pipe.
"They never seem to bother me," he'd say.
"You ought to try prevention just a bit."
She'd make a face, then laugh, but did not stir;
And so they spent dessert time of their day,
Mere taste of pleasure savored as they shared.
Their condiment, thus utilized, was served
In portions less by far than they deserved.

————Mary R. Palmer

THE NURSING HOME

The CNA brings in my tray
A cheery smile to start the day.
The cook has made a special treat
Perhaps some eggs or cream of wheat.

An aide shows up to bathe and dress
Another picks up last night's mess.
A nurse stops by to sit and chat
One has my pills—I don't like that!!

A while goes by I sit outside
Then someone takes me for a ride.
I look in all the rooms and then
A helper takes me back again.

Someone comes in to check my air
Another helps me to my chair.
Sometimes a friend stops in and stays
Until they bring the supper trays.

I do not like to be here now
I'd rather be at home somehow
But since I'm here I have to say
The people here just make my day!!

———Vivian Spruce

FIRST ENCOUNTER

I was with grandma when the telegram came.
As she read, she sobbed my uncle's name.
To hide her tears, she buried her head,
I wondered what the telegram said.
At four, I knew nothing of war and dying.
It hurt so to have my grandma crying.
I kissed her arms and brushed her hair,
But it seemed as if I were not there.
I ran outside, hoping to get her
A bunch of flowers to make her feel better.
Red devil's paintbrush is what I found
And weak-stemmed yellow hawkweed all around.
Clutching them firmly, I raced back to see
If she would stop weeping and smile at me.
Grief raised her hand and pushed me away,
Rejecting me and my poor bouquet.
What color is sorrow?
Mine's red and yellow.

———Vivian Spruce

ABOUT THE CONTRIBUTORS

ERNESTINE F. BENT, Plymouth, Maine, loved and wrote poetry since childhood without preserving her manuscripts. In 1954 Julia "Bunny" Ward suggested she join the Poetry Fellowship. Then things began to change! (Pages 63, 64)

JEAN BLODGETT, Brownville, Maine, is a seventy-five year old housewife who loves writing and learning something new every day. (Pages 24, 49)

SHARON BRAY, Orland, Maine, is a writer, editor and community health education activist. She publishes *Narramissic Notebook* twice a year. (Pages 14, 69)

JEANETTE K. CAKOUROS, Woolwich, is a Maine native whose award-winning reviews, essays and feature articles have been published in magazines and newspapers across the country. (Page 17)

EARLENE AHLQUIST "KITTY" CHADBOURNE, Cumberland Center, Maine, of Scandinavian heritage, was raised in Scarborough. A mother, grandmother, archivist, she is president of our Society. *The most memorable stories are those in poetic form.* (Pages 8, 30)

ERIK CHRISTIAN, Dagsboro, Delaware, received a Master's degree from the University of New Hampshire, has worked in developmental disabilities, in prisons, private practice and as adjunct professor. (Page 40)

ROBERT M. CHUTE, Brunswick, Maine, is a native of Naples educated at Fryeburg Academy, University of Maine at Orono, Johns Hopkins. Writing since age fourteen, he has appeared in a wide variety of journals and published nine chapbooks. (Pages 31, 70)

H. R. COURSEN, Brunswick, Maine. His thirtieth book of poetry, *An Old Song,* and his twenty-second novel, *The Blind Prophet of Archerland,* recently appeared from Mathom and Goose River respectively. He was professor of English at Bowdoin College for thirty years. (Pages 9, 87)

YAMILE CRAVEN, Concord, New Hampshire, has won poetry contests, been published in anthologies and magazines, brought out four chapbooks, and has earned a degree in English literature. (Pages 52, 80)

DAVID LEWELLYN DAVIS, Orland, Maine, watches all the seasons in a place he loves alongside the Narramissic River. *The urge is to write poetry so I do.* (Pages 65, 66)

INA DOBAN, Camden, Maine, grew up in the Midwest, and moved east after marriage. She and her husband have lived in Camden for seventeen years. (Pages 27, 53)

ROSALIE DOUGHTY, Bucksport, Maine, has been a wife for forty-eight years, mother of three, grandmother of eight, great-grandmother of three. Past officer of five organizations and a current officer in two. *Slow now, but busy.* (Pages 59, 60)

VICTORIA EASTMAN, Milo, Maine, lives with her husband and little boy. She teaches adults creative writing, has organized writers fairs, and established several writing groups. She is also an artist. (Pages 51, 58)

MARGARET ROCKWELL FINCH, Bath, Maine, was born in New Jersey, 1921. Spent countless summers in Maine; moved here in 1998. Poet for eighty years: published in magazines, anthologies. One collection, *Davy's Lake* (1996). (Pages 74, 79)

ANNE W. HAMMOND, Bath, Maine. Business woman, environmental educator, hiker. Produced three videos on the Androscoggin-Kennebec watershed. Paddled a kayak over 3000 miles, mostly in Maine. Published in anthology, *Untidy Candles* (1995). (Pages 15, 88)

LEE HUTCHINS, Bayonet Point, Florida, lived twenty-four years in Maine. Teaches English and creative writing. Published in previous Maine Poets Society anthologies, magazines; has a chapbook, *Puzzle Pieces*. (Pages 3, 37)

SALLY R. JOY, Augusta, Maine, lives with her husband, Lt. Col. John F. Joy, (US Army Retired). She works full time as a word processor operator. (Pages 25, 84)

SHANDI KENNEDY-ROBERTSON, Chelsea, Maine, was recently voted Poet Laureate of Cony High School by teachers and peers. Back-up singer for her mother, she's forming a band with friends. Desires to attend Columbia College in 2006. (Pages 5, 6)

HELEN STREETER KELLY, Dover-Foxcroft, Maine (transplanted from Cape Cod, Massachusetts), writes for the pleasure of language, the impact of words, and the music they create. (Pages 47, 48)

BETTY KING, Woolwich, Maine, lives on a hard-scrabble farm on the inland waterway between Bath and Boothbay Harbor. She has seven grown children, a husband, and a dog. (Pages 23, 71)

JUNE A. KNOWLES, Belmont, Massachusetts, published poet in magazines, anthologies, newspapers, and self-published collections. Reads for a variety of audiences. Several leadership roles (1976-2001) with State of Maine Writers Conference. (1999-2001 Conference co-chair). (Pages 18, 36)

ANN MACKINNON KUCERA, Garland, Maine, was Massachusetts raised. Milkmaid, accountant, college student, English teacher, in that order. Attended seven colleges; MA English. Published three novels, six chapbooks, one local history. (Pages 7, 81)

ANITA LIBERTY, Alfred, Maine, lives with her husband, Bob. They have two sons and two grandsons. *My poetry describes my love of my native Maine.* (Pages 72, 89)

PAUL AVERILL LIEBOW, MD, FACEP, Bucksport, Maine. EMMC career ED Physician for almost 30 years. Maine EMS Regional Medical Director. VP of NRCM. Maine delegate to NWF. Maine PSR activist of the year. (Page 42)

BILL LINDIE, Waterville, Maine, retired military and Honorary Poet Laureate of Doughty Bog and Eighteen Ridge, sits and watches the seasons come—and go—from a mid-Maine bungalow. (Page 26, 85)

ROBIN MERRILL, born in Farmington, Maine, where she continues to live. She is Third Mate in the Merchant Marine and a Great Lakes Pilot. (Pages 4, 16)

EARLA TOWNE NELSON, Brownville, Maine, member of Poetry Fellowship and Maine Poets Society thirty years, held many offices, now Round Robin Secretary. Published in three anthologies and Sebec Historical Quarterly. (Pages 35, 75)

DEBORAH NEUMEISTER, RN, Oakland, Maine, 53, mother of two, has written poetry since she was sixteen, lived in Maine most of her life, joined the Society twelve years ago. (Pages 13, 50)

ARNOLD PERRIN, Union, Maine, a Pushcart Prize nominee, 1994, poetry editor of the New England Sampler, editor-publisher of Wings Press. Published widely in journals, author of five books including *Window* (Talent House Press, 1998). (Pages 10, 29)

JOYCE PYE, Bath, a native of Maine, is an author and poet. Her work, published in Maine and Ireland, includes *Ireland's Musical Instrument Makers.* (Pages 82, 83)

BERNARD RYER, Fairfield, Maine. "Red" has been writing poems for about fifteen years and has put out several collections. He recently passed his eighty-ninth birthday. (Pages 57, 73)

JAMES B. SARGENT, Auburn, Maine, watches the Androscoggin flow by his home of sixty-plus years. *Sometimes I wonder how much has gotten past me without my even thinking about it.* Lifelong farmer, biologist, former research assistant, Jackson Laboratory. (Pages 19, 39)

WALTER FIELD SARGENT, Auburn, Maine (father of James). DOB 1/11/11. Entered UMO 1930 (hasn't graduated yet) but has been a member of Maine Poets Society for 50+ years. (Pages 76, 86)

LORNA STARBIRD, Brockton, Massachusetts. Her hometown is Lisbon Falls, Maine. Member of Maine Poets Society since 1947. Attended Maine Writers Conference from 1948 to mid 1990's. (Pages 28, 38)

JULIA "BUNNY" WARD, Pittsfield, Maine, is in her ninety-second year. Poet since high school; joined the Poetry Fellowship (which became Maine Poets Society) in 1953 after moving to Maine. *I wish you all the joy I have found down through the years. Cheers!* (Pages 61, 62)

POSTHUMOUS BIOGRAPHICAL NOTES

MARY HELEN GEORGITIS (1921-2002) was born in Milbridge, Maine, educated at Westbrook Junior College and Mount Holyoke. She was also a painter, and taught English at Orono High School over the years. (Pages 93, 94)

MARY RUTH PALMER (1922-2002), born in Buxton, lifelong resident of Maine, mother, teacher, diverse and prolific author, president of Maine Poets Society. Widely published, several poetry books, recently a memoir of her childhood farm days, *Kid Sisters Never Forget: Remembering the Great Depression.* (Dedication Page and Page 95)

VIVIAN D. SPRUCE, (1914-2002) lived in Orono, Maine. Retired from teaching and postal work, she began writing poetry in her eighties. *A lifelong lover of words as a natural outlet for her very active mind.* (Pages 96, 97)

CREDITS & ACKNOWLEDGMENTS

H. R. Coursen: "April" will appear in *Maine Seasons,* Just Write Books, 2005.

Lee Hutchins: "Center Moriches 1941" is from *Puzzle Pieces,* C.M. Free Public Library, N.D.

Sally R. Joy: "Victory" and "Potential" appeared in *Science of Mind,* May 1977, June 1978.

Shandi Kennedy-Robertson: "Not Another 'Sappy' Love Poem" appeared In *Tracing the Infinite,* International Library of Poetry, N.D.

Ann Kucera: "Treasure" appeared in *The High Intemperance,* Holts Mill Press, Garland, Maine, 2000.

Robin Merrill: "dining in" appeared in *Creosote,* N.D. "Languages" in *River King Poetry Supplement,* N.D.

Mary R. Palmer: "The Condiment" appeared in *Kid Sisters Never Forget,* Buxton-Hollis Historical Society, 2002.

Arnold Perrin: "Hoya Plant" was published in *Live Poets Society Series,* 1993 (Post Cards)

David L. Davis: "Alphabet Seed" and "When" were printed in *Sense & Place* and *Ready to Be Surprised,* and *H.O.M.E. Words,* N.D.

Earlene Ahlquist Chadbourne: "Quietude" and "Reappearances" were published in *The Pearl Collection,* 1997.

The editors would like to acknowledge the typing and editing contribution of Helen Streeter Kelly, without whose skills this volume might still be in the works.

INDEX

Printed in the United States
34723LVS00006B/313-501

9 780976 653332